The Volcano King

Jahvon Flowers,
Rhovon Flowers & Rhoan Flowers

Copyright * 2020   Rhoan Flowers
All rights reserved. Except as permitted under (U.S Copyright Act of 1976), or (Canadian Copyright Act of 2012), no part of this publication may be reproduced, distributed, or transmitted in any form or by any means, or stored in a database or retrieval system, without the prior written permission of the publisher.

ISBN 978-1-9991642-2-5
ISBN 978-1-9991642-0-1

Written By: Rhoan Flowers Artwork By: Rhovon Flowers & Jahvon Flowers
Cover By: Clyde Williams www.graphiquemezza.com
Book Layout By: www.bookdesign.ca

GRAPHIQUE
MEZZA

It was a remarkably dark night at The Academy Developmental School, and all the students, and professors, were passed out inside their dorm rooms. The tiger on guard throughout the institution, were accustomed to quiet nights on the job, and would idle about instead of adequately protecting their posts. The two guards at the front gate of the enclosed compound, were dozing off, when the sound from a broken twig, awoke one of them. There was an invading unit of black panthers hidden among the trees, but the weary eyed guard saw nothing troubling, and resumed his nap. Both guards were sound asleep moments later, when the panthers moved in and overpowered them. All the tiger guards were easily captured by the panthers, who chained them to each other, before they proceeded to terrorize the students and professors.

There was once unity among the numerous species, that resided on the Island of Naganoo. Most of the tiger residents in the largest village of Kamoo, spent very little time with their offspring, and would have monkeys tend to them from they were babies. The youngsters would grow through animal cares systems, until they got sent away to the private learning institution, at the ages of five until eleven. Whenever the uniquely built brown wagon, and lead zebra from The Academy arrived in the village, there was always a lineup of parents eagerly waiting to register their youngsters. There was also a second lineup of parents, who were eagerly expecting their children, or whatever news there was of their status. The wagon was sparklingly clean and had one occupant, which was an old monkey who had a long white beard. The old monkey slowly dismounted from the wagon, then addressed the parents who were expecting their young ones to return, after they had completed the notable institution.

"Hello, my dear parents," pleasantly greeted the old monkey, after he finished assembling a small table, with a few black boxes!

"Oh, how is my boy James, Headmaster Knuckleberry," asked the first female monkey in line?

"Look into this cube, and see and hear for yourself Miss Baxley," calmly answered Headmaster Knuckleberry, who handed the female a black cube from his table!

"Hello, Headmaster Knuckleberry, our daughter Peaches should have been home months ago, is there any word from her," asked the next mother in line?

"Oh, Mrs. Petgrave, Peaches continues to be one of the hardest working pupils at the Academy! Hear from her for yourself," said Headmaster Knuckleberry, who passed her and everyone else in line a similar cube!

As the parents looked into the black cubes, they each saw happy videos of their children, who spoke to them and assured them, 'they were thoroughly looked after, while they enjoyed their new learning environment.

Once the enquiring parents left, the old monkey turned to the parents waiting to register their young ones.

"Hello everyone, I am Headmaster Knuckleberry from the Academy Developmental Institution! I take it you are all here to register your little ones," asked the old monkey?

"We sure are! Hello, my name is Sue, and this is our son Denny; and we would like to register him into your academy," asked the lady at the front of the line?

"Hello Denny, welcome to The Academy of Hard Work! Say your goodbyes, then climb on the wagon please," Headmaster Knuckleberry stated?

Denny was not too pleased about being shipped off like so many others from their village, so instead of saying goodbye to his parents, he angrily climbed onto the wagon. The second parents signed up their child Zoah the tigress; and agreed to have the school keep her 'for as long as they decreed it necessary'. There were less enrollments than Headmaster Knuckleberry usually collected, but the small toll of four new bodies were equally welcomed.

As soon as the wagon was out of the villagers' sights, a drastic transformation occurred onboard. Zoah and the other recruits were unexpectedly bound with metal restraints, that appeared from nowhere, and secured their hooves and legs to the floor.

"Hey, what is the meaning of this," Denny demanded!?

"Headmaster Knuckleberry, why are there chains holding us down," Zoah asked?

"Yeah, you better let us go right now," Taz added!

The wagon vanished into the thick green forest and reemerged moments later, at an unrecognizable section of the island. Well beyond the thick barrier of trees was an empty stretch of land, that extended for as far as the eyes could see. The once flourishing forest had been stripped of all its trees, vegetation, birds, and animals, which used to cover the entire island. With all the transformations, one of the largest was Headmaster Knuckleberry, whose long white beard turned red, to match the color of his cape.
"Knoxberry," Taz declared!
"How nice of you to have heard of me! But for those of you who don't know who I am; from this moment forth, you will refer to me as Sorcerer Knoxberry," threatened the old monkey!
"What do you want with us," Taz enquired?
"Oh, a lot my young worker. You are all going to do some hard-physical labor! I guarantee you that," Sorcerer Knoxberry answered!
(picture 6: Headmaster Knoxberry standing before the prisoners on the wagon)

The newcomers were all surprised to see the demolition operation underway, which included huge machinery with sharp blades, that devoured everything in their path. As the wagon passed by the workers, who left nothing but unfertile soil in their wake, tears rolled from Zoah's eyes, as they watched their village mates toiled under constant pressure. The wizard had a very sophisticated operation and, got free labor from the Academy's students and professors, who all appeared to be under some sort of mind control. Sorcerer Knoxberry had an army of black panthers and several brown monkeys in his employment, who all ensured the captives worked and obeyed orders.

"Admiral Tusk, have some of your guards process those new workers! Then tell General Zy, I would like to have a word in my study," Sorcerer Knoxberry ordered a panther on his way to his private tent!

"Right away Sorcerer Knoxberry," Admiral Tusk responded!

The instant Denny, Taz, Zoah, and Merv, got taken off the wagon, four panthers led them to a tent for orientation. While being led to the tent, Zoah was shocked to see her brother, who was hard at work like everyone else.

"Xander! It's me Zoah, your little sister," Zoah said to the worker, who did not even look in her direction, but continued his duties.

"Silence, there will be no talking with the workers," said a guard, who electrocuted Zoah with an electric zapper!

"Ouch, that really hurts," Zoah stated?

"You, get inside there and watch the screen for orientation," a guard ordered Merv, who was first in line!

General Zy, Admiral Tusk, and Sorcerer Knoxberry had a strategic meeting inside the wizard's personal tent. The meeting was held to discuss their strategy against members of their own invasion team.

"Once we have entrapped the tigers of Kamoo, we will have no further use for Gybba and his wild boar associates! So, I want you to take him out, General Zy," Sorcerer Knoxberry indicated!

"It is a well-known fact that the boars don't trust me! So, how am I supposed to get close to Gybba," General Zy asked?

"Admiral Tusk here will have to do the honors then! During the negotiations, I want you to sneak behind the boars with some of our troops; and take out Gybba whenever you get a chance! If we eliminate their leader, then handling the rest of those boars should be quite easy," Sorcerer Knoxberry stated!

"Sorcerer Knoxberry, the boars have a large army, what if we can't get to Gybba," Admiral Tusk enquired?

"I have our engineers working on a machine that will tilt this battle in our favor! If I must, then I will use that if necessary," Sorcerer Knoxberry responded!

After their discussion terminated, and the general and his admiral were on their way from the tent, Sorcerer Knoxberry stopped them and demanded that, 'Tusk stayed behind for a few minutes'?

"Did you see what that device did to Merv? That's how everybody got to be like that," Denny stated!
"But I don't want to be like them! What are we going to do," Taz whispered?
"Whatever they tell you to do inside there, don't do it! If they tell you to look, close your eyes; and here, stuff some of this in your ears," Zoah suggested, as she slipped him some fur!
"If this works, what do we do after we get out of there," Denny asked?
"Make sure you move and act like the workers do. Then we join Merv's crew and stay together," Zoah whispered!
"Hey, you get in there now," commanded the guard!

Sorcerer Knoxberry went into the Invention Tent with General Zy, where he had several monkeys working on a secret project. General Zy was the leader of Knoxberry's panther army, and a sworn ally to the wizard, who also had him under mind control. There were two guards posted by the entrance to hinder anyone from entering, who was not a member of Knoxberry's inner circle.

"Have you engineers gotten this contraption working yet," Knoxberry yelled?

"Not quite Sir, but we are very close," answered the primary engineer!

"We will be at my enemies' doorstep in four days! So, make sure this machine is ready to go by then, or you will all pay the consequences," Knoxberry threatened!

"We will not disappoint you Sorcerer Knoxberry," responded the same engineer!

"I pray you do not, or you will certainly not live to see the next day," Sorcerer Knoxberry warned, before he stormed out with General Zy!

That night in camp Zoah, Taz, and Denny gathered to discuss their options. Following such a long and tough day, almost every other captive was passed out from fatigue, except for Jax, who earlier observed some subtle differences in the newcomers; and had been secretly monitoring them since.

"Hey guys! I'm so happy to see you all passed orientation," Jax whispered, yet startled the newcomers!

"Oh my gosh Jax, you almost gave me a heart attack," Denny said!

"Cousin Jax, I'm so happy you are not under that mind control! What is Sorcerer Knoxberry planning to do," Taz whisperingly asked?

"He says he wants to get revenge for the panthers, by killing or enslaving everyone in our village! But I believe he also has another plan, though I don't know what that is yet," Jax answered.

"Then why are they destroying the forest," Zoah demanded?

"To collect all the Solar Hibiscus Plants across the island. Knoxberry have found a way to create the energy they use to do everything. Like power up those zappers they used to electrocute you," Jax responded!

"That thing really hurt! It almost knocked me out," Zoah stated!

"We all know the largest quantity of Solar Hibiscus Plants are in Kamoo, so we have to escape from here! Has anyone ever successfully gotten away," Taz asked?

"I'm afraid not my friend! The forest between us and our home is guarded by the wild boars, and the barren lands behind us leads directly to the sea! No one ever tried to escape and returned," Jax whispered!

There were three tents on the wizard's compound, the first and largest was used by his guards for their sleeping and dining purposes, the second his personal quarters, and the third was his restricted facility, where they engineered secret weapons. The residents of Kamoo had no idea their forest was receding, and they were on the verge of being invaded. Sorcerer Knoxberry used his magic to create a humongous mirror, that casted the illusion of an extended forest beyond the tigers' borders, while his slaves demolished the trees at a rapid pace. Each morning prior to the rise of the sun, the sorcerer from inside his personal quarters would use energy from the Solar Hibiscus Plants they collected, to construct the illusion mirror. Once night fell over the island, the mirror would automatically disappear, but by then it was impossible for the Kamoo villagers to see beyond the tall trees.

The next day Jax and three other monkeys, were ordered to remove the waste bin from the Invention Tent. When they entered the tent, Jax and his associates were ordered to collect the garbage off the floor, and finish loading the bin, before they emptied it behind the camp. Jax had never seen the secret machine being built, and was stunned at the mechanics, and size of the humongous machine, however, he had to suppress his astonishment to avoid being detected. There were two engineers discussing what they needed to complete, for the machine to be ready within the next three days, when they were estimated to reach the Kamoo village.

While completing his chores, Jax spotted a small red device on a table that appeared important, so he stole it. The monkeys brought the bin out and emptied it, then returned it to the tent's entrance, where a panther took charge, and brought it back inside. The treatment assessed to the kidnaped villagers was harsh, considering they were forced to endure the outdoor elements, whether the sun blazed across the sky, or rain drenched the turf. The panthers did their best to break and weaken their captives, by giving them the bare minimal necessary to survive. Water, food, and rest were shortened to drain the workers' strength, even though they were already under mind control.

There was no need for tight security around the camp, with the captives under the mind control effects. Everyone was accounted for each morning, which was the only time the guards counted the workers. Later that night after all the other captives had fallen asleep, the four mutineers gathered for their nightly conference. The guards would pass by once every few hours to check, therefore, they had to keep watch and listen to ensure they were not caught.

"We must escape tonight," Jax whispered!

"Wait, I thought you said nobody ever got away safely," Taz argued?

"In a few days they are going to reach our home; and I've seen the machine they plan to use to capture our parents," Jax stated!

"So how are we supposed to get by the wild boars? And if we can't, where will we go," Taz asked?

"I don't know," Jax responded.

"The only thing that can help us escape all this craziness is the Volcano King," Denny said, as he stared up at the summit of Mont Plymouth, which was the highest peak on Naganoo Island!

"Volcano who," Taz questioned?

"For the last time Denny, that is only a myth, told to you by your dead grandfather," Zoah answered!

"And I told you it's not a myth! My grandfather would never lie to me; and he said, 'if I must run away one day, then run to the top of the volcano mountain instead of the sea'," Denny stated.

"That won't be necessary! I think we might be able to run around the wild boars and get back to Kamoo. Get ready to go, we leave after the next guards pass," Jax instructed!

Early that morning, the engineers inside the Invention Tent, completed Knoxberry's secret weapon, and wanted to test it before daybreak. The machine was a giant robot that could be operated by a monkey, who would climb into the operator's station and handle the controls. The main engineer Dr. Flux climbed into the conductor's station, and pressed the engage button, but nothing happened. The engineer again pressed the button and was dejected, before he realized there was an important element missing.
"Where is the Energizer Core," Dr. Flux asked?
"Oh, sorry doc, I placed it on the table over there for safety," said another engineer, who went to recover the device. "But I can't find it, it's gone!"
"What! Who could have taken that thing," pondered Dr. Flux for a while? "Those Kamoo monkeys who emptied the trash earlier; find them!

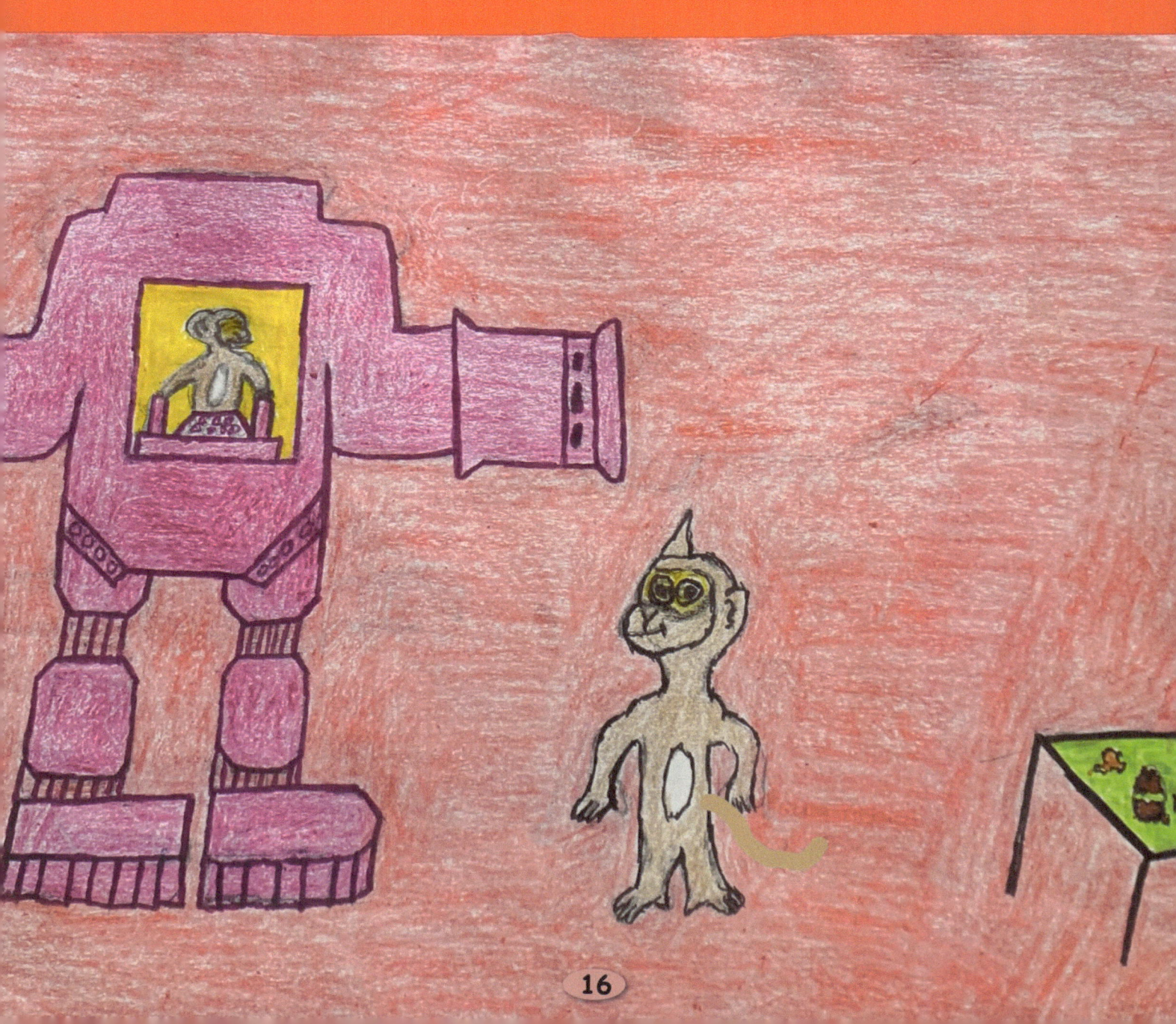

It wasn't until the guards went to search for Jax and his cleaning associates, that they noticed there were four captives missing. Whistles began blowing throughout the compound, as the guards surrounded their captives, to ascertain exactly who had ran off. Once they determined who was missing, General Zy went to inform Sorcerer Knoxberry, but had to wait until the wizard finished installing their illusion mirror before he disturbed him. While the general patiently waited outside, Dr. Flux nervously arrived to disclose the disappointing news.
"What is that infernal racket out there, General Zy," Knoxberry demanded once they entered his tent?
"Three new captives and a student escaped Sorcerer Knoxberry," General Zy answered!
"A-a-a-and I'm afraid, that one of them might have taken your Energizer Core for your robot suit, Sir," Dr. Flux nervously added.
"What," Knoxberry shouted! "Have them prepare my wagon General Zy!"

Sorcerer Knoxberry, General Zy, and four of their guards visited the wild boar Gybba in the forest. Knoxberry rode his trusted zebra with General Zy alongside him, while their security guards followed behind. The panthers and the wild boars had a long stretch of bad history, therefore the black cats and their brown coat nemesis, grunted and roared at each other when they first encountered. However, once Knoxberry and Gybba began their talks, everyone seized the hostilities.

"We will be in Kamoo by the next two days, and I don't foresee our victory coming much longer after that," Sorcerer Knoxberry stated.

"What do you want us wild boars to do during the invasion," Gybba asked?

"When we arrive, I shall have no use of your services, so you and your troops can guard the western section of the village, where I don't expect much resistance," Sorcerer Knoxberry instructed!

"But you said we would equally share the victory," Gybba said?

"This will be all our victory! But in the mean time I have an urgent job for you to handle! Four of our workers ran away last night, and one of them has a core I want you to recover, before you dispose of them," Sorcerer Knoxberry ordered!

"Don't worry Sorcerer, they are as good as dead," Gybba stated!

The four escapees were cautiously advancing along the edge of the forest, when Denny overheard something approaching in the distance. To ensure there was no eminent danger, Taz quickly climbed a tall tree to look off in the distance. As soon as Taz climbed to a decent height, he began quickly descending from the tree, after he saw the army of wild boars racing toward them.

"The wild boars are coming directly at us," Taz yelled!

"Which direction are they coming from," Zoah asked?

"They are scattered across the forest, so if we continue straight it's only a matter of time before we run into them! We can either go back or head up to the top of the volcano, but whatever the decision, we must do it now," Taz declared!

"If we go back, we will certainly get recaptured, so we have no choice but to head up the mountain," Denny responded!

"Up the mountain; let's go," Jax declared!

The wild boars were remarkably fast and began gaining ground on the fleeing captives. The monkeys' slow speed was compromising the escape efforts, considering they moved slower than their predators. With the wild boars getting ever closer, Zoah and Denny had no choice but to throw both monkeys on their backs, and carried them up the steep slope. Zoah assumed the wild boars would give up the chase, due to the massive climb up Mont Plymouth, but nothing would discourage the vigilantes who were ordered to return the stolen item.

"Why are these wild boars so persistent, they are usually scared of heights," Zoah stated?

"That might have something to do with this thing that I stole from Sorcerer Knoxberry's invention tent," Jax responded, as he showed his companions the Energizer Core.

"What the hell is that," Denny asked?

"I don't know! It looked important, so I grabbed it," Jax responded!

When Zoah, Chase, Denny, and Jax reached the summit of Mont Plymouth, they quickly looked around for another way off the mountain. Realizing there was no other option, the group gathered at the ledge of the volcano, and looked inside for a safe way to escape.
"Oh no we're trapped, what are we going to do," Zoah declared?
"Guys, we might have just locked ourselves in the worst corner possible. They might just throw us all inside the volcano to get rid of us," Jax stated!
"Oh, great Volcano King, could you please help us," Denny said, as he stared down into the fiery abyss?
"Enough with this Volcano King, we're in real trouble! Anyone else have any ideas," Taz argued?

Deep inside the volcano in his private study, the Volcano King overheard the words of the terrified escapees. It was the king's obligation to help anyone in distress, therefore he left his quarters and went out for a firsthand encounter. Some of the wild boars had climbed to the top of the mountain, and were intent on following Knoxberry's orders, by throwing the escaped workers into the volcano. Sighting the danger, the Volcano King waved his right paw, at which sectional ledges began appearing all throughout the inner walls of the volcano.

"Look, ledges like steps for us to go down," Denny pointed out, before he began jumping from one ledge to the next!

Gybba smiled to himself, as he watched the runaways voluntarily jumped into the volcano. The leader of the wild boars slowly walked to the edge of the volcano, and looked in, expecting to see charred bodies dissolving in the boiling lava below. To his astonishment, Knoxberry's workers were safely escaping on invisible ledges, that Gybba could not see. By the time the other wild boars reached the volcano's edge, all the escapees had disappeared into a tunnel, therefore, Gybba pretended as if they all perished, then led his troops back to ground level.

The escapees nervously walked through a tunnel, with small lumps of lava burning fire to provide light. At the end of the tunnel was a private room with one occupant, who was the Volcano King.
"Wow, I told them you existed," Denny said!
"It appears that you are all in search of refuge," Volcano King asked?
"Yes, we need serious help," Jax exclaimed!
"Why were you being chased by the boars," Volcano King questioned?
"They are working for this Sorcerer Knoxberry, who intends to destroy this entire island," Zoah answered!
"Knoxberry, what is he up to now," Volcano King declared?
"Do you know Sorcerer Knoxberry," Zoah asked?
"More than half a century ago Knoxberry washed up on our shores, after he was exiled from his homeland on the Island of Mukie. Since then he had vowed to return to Mukie and have his revenge against those who sentenced him, no matter the cost! All the species on Naganoo lived in harmony before this wizard came here and disrupted everything. The panthers, tigers, monkeys, and every other creature lived as one, until Knoxberry's grand plague, which was a sickness he invented and used to divide everyone." King Volcano explained.
"Since you know all this, and how evil Knoxberry is, then you must help us," Denny reasoned!?
"You are all tired and weary from your travels, go and take a nap, and we will discuss this matter when you awaken," King Volcano declared!

While his visitors slept, King Volcano went to the peak of his mountain and looked down in the valley. The king walked around the ledge of Mont Plymouth and surveyed the land beneath, which was victimized of its trees, vegetation, and livestock. King Volcano had not left his domain in years; therefore, he had no idea of the destruction and cruelty being awarded to some of the locals. Much of the island was like a lifeless desert, from the base of Mont Plymouth to the boundaries of the sea. The devastation was shocking and angered the king, who charged back into his domain, then locked himself inside his private suite. A fiery orb engulfed the Volcano King, who even exhaled fire as he puffed with rage. With the king deeply outraged, the lava inside the volcano gradually began bubbling, and slowly rose to the surface.
"Mr. Volcano King… Mr. Volcano King, can I please come in," Jax called out?
To calm his temper, the Volcano King began thinking of his guests, and his obligation to them. The lava inside the pit was halfway up the mountain's inner walls, when the king regained control of his emotions, at which the boiling fluid began slowly receding to the bottom.

Gybba and some of his followers walked into Sorcerer Knoxberry's camp, where several of the panthers growled at them as they passed by. The wild boars, who were usually feisty against the panthers, were more subdued amid the pack of black cats.

"Ah, my loyal followers, what news have you brought me," Sorcerer Knoxberry asked?

"We did as you commanded and got rid of those pesky runaways, but we were unable to recover your Energizer Core," Gybba exclaimed!

"What do you mean you were unable to recover the core," Sorcerer Knoxberry yelled?

"Well Sir, after I threw the first one into the volcano, the rest of them feared me doing the same and voluntarily jumped in," Gybba explained!

"That will affect my grand scheme this time, but luckily we have everything we need to bring our enemies to their knees! Tell Dr. Flux to make sure he replaces the lost core, before our next mission," Sorcerer Knoxberry threatened, as he looked over at the young captives!

Jax was the first to awaken and curiously walked into the library, where the Volcano King had calmed down, and was back to his normal self. The monkey was concerned about the king's wellbeing and wanted to know why he chose such a boring existence.

"Have you always been alone here," Jax asked?

The Volcano King was at first hesitant to respond, but eventually answered. "No, there was a time when I taught certain creatures of this island."

"And what happened," Jax continued?

"The island wide separation by Knoxberry, made it impossible for me to teach any one species, over the next, so my teaching days ended," Volcano King stated.

"Are you not bored being here alone all these years, and what do you do all day," Jax enquired?

"There is no time for boredom when you spend your time doing what motivates you! And studying the universe is what drives me," Volcano King explained!

"Did you write all these books," Jax asked?

"Yes, I have documented everything I've learnt about our galaxy all these years," Volcano King replied!

"Wow! All this knowledge," Jax said, as she picked up a book and started reading it.

The Volcano King looked at the monkey and reminisced about times past, when he taught the locals lessons. But he did not realize he missed teaching as much, until he saw Jax scrolling through the book.

Denny, Zoah, and Taz joined their host and Jax inside the library, eager to hear what the Volcano King's decision was. Jax had warmed up quite nicely to the Volcano King by then, so much that they were overheard giggling down the hall.

"Excuse us Volcano King, but have you decided if you will help us get rid of this wizard," Zoah asked?

"I believe you were all led here for a reason; and speaking with Jax here have made it quite clear... You were all sent here to serve as survivors for your families," Volcano King stated.

"What! No! We were on our way to help our families survive this tyrant," Taz argued!

"Yes, you were! But faith drove you all here to survive my response to this crisis! And that is the destruction of everything on Naganoo Island," Volcano King declared!

"No way, you can't do that," Denny exclaimed!

"I am sorry, but I am not allowed to serve as a one-sided judge. The Island of Naganoo is under great treat and I must cleanse and retain all its assets! Therefore, I will rain lava on everything beneath my mountain, this is my final judgement," Volcano King declared!

"Before you cast your judgement, you have to give us a chance to save our families? Please," Jax begged?

"I shall give you one chance to save your loved ones, but if you fail, I will destroy everything on this island," Volcano King stated, as he retrieved, and passed them a golden trumpet! "Blow this horn in the midst of these fighters, then warn everyone of what will come if this war persists!"

The warning bells, which had not sounded in the Village of Kamoo for decades, began ringing early on the morning of the invasion. All the male guardians reported to the front of their village, while the females protected the youngest among them. The Kamoo monkeys' and tigers' defensive team was led by General Brut, who stood before his guardians and watched, as the last trees across their borderline got demolished by Knoxberry's huge machines.

The day finally came when Sorcerer Knoxberry refrained from installing their illusion mirror, while his troops prepared for combat. The panthers were outnumbered by the tigers, who all showed their anger at the atrocity committed, by roaring at their invaders. All the beautiful scenery and sounds of the forest were gone, and there was no way to repair the damage, hence the locals wanted to rip their island contenders apart. With their adversaries viciously roaring and taunting to attack, Sorcerer Knoxberry instructed his troops, 'to tie the young captives to the front of their huge machines'. The tigers' aggressions immediately simmered, when they looked across the battlefield at their own offspring, being used as a ploy.

"What have you done with the staff of the Academy," General Brut asked?

"Let's just say, we worked them to death," General Zy responded!

"You will all surrender; or watch as your young ones get torn to shreds!" Sorcerer Knoxberry instructed!

"Our tribes have not agreed since the days of our fathers. But never would we ever consider enslaving your offspring, or using them as pawns on the battlefield," General Brut argued!

Zoah and the others were shown a way out of the volcano, through a tunnel that led directly to their village. When they reached the western side of the battlefield, there was no way through with the wild boars blocking their path, therefore, Jax blew the horn, which immediately caught everyone's attention. Every islander except the wizard, knew to succumb to the instruction provided thereafter, thus, a platform had to be provided for the horn's holder to speak. The wild boars respectively parted ways, and allowed the four escapees to walk through, to address everyone on the field. Jax again blew the horn, as they passed between the army of boars.

"The Horn of Naganoo!" General Brut and others in his company recited.
"The Horn of Naganoo!" Gybba and others in his company recited.
"The Horn of Naganoo!" General Zy and others in his army recited.
"What is that deafening sound in my ears," Sorcerer Knoxberry asked?
"The most mystical instrument on this island. Legend says, it was used by the Volcano King to transmit his final warning," General Zy answered!
"I was sent by the Volcano King, to issue this one and only warning! To you, invaders, return to your lands and end this war immediately, or I shall unleash boiling lava, and destroy everything on this island," Jax declared!

Everyone looked to Sorcerer Knoxberry for him to make the final determination and terminate their attack. Even though both the sorcerer's associates and their nemesis were confident about what would transpire, Knoxberry believed the entire warning was a trick, hence, he had no plans to terminate their mission. With everyone extremely frightful of the outcome, the wizard played on their emotional state, and used his cunning to gain ultimate control.

"Bring me this Horn of Naganoo, so I can check its authenticity, to be sure of this prophesy," Sorcerer Knoxberry reasoned!?

Gybba and several of his troops surrounded the four news bearers and brought them to the wizard. Jax was happy to hand over the Golden Trumpet, for Sorcerer Knoxberry and his followers to evaluate, and realize they spoke the truth. Instead of inspecting the instrument's authenticity, the wizard simply tossed it on the ground, and ordered the wild boars 'to secure and search the returned escapees'! One of the wild boars retrieved the Energizer Core from Jax and gave it to the sorcerer's chief engineer. Dr. Flux loaded the Energizer Core, into the machine built for Knoxberry, before the wizard climbed aboard and continued with his tyranny.

"There will be no escape for any of you; and no one will be coming to your rescue," Sorcerer Knoxberry threatened, as he began using the personally built robot to cast restraints at the Kamoo villagers!

The Volcano King watched and became infuriated after his warning went unheeded. As the king grew increasingly angry, the lava inside the volcano began boiling, and slowly rose to the top. While the sorcerer attacked with his machine, an explosion sounded that sent huge boulders of heated lava, shooting some twenty kilometers into the air. The terrifying sight made the female tigers scream in horror, so many grabbed their offspring and began running toward the ocean. A frantic scramble took place, where most of the combatants took off running, with their eyes to the sky. The boiling lava eventually reached its peak, then began running down from all sides of the mountain, toward the village and elsewhere. Knoxberry had immobilized General Brut and was in the process of immobilizing several other tigers, when he heard the explosion and noticed the impending danger.

A huge fiery bolder came falling from the sky and crashed into the ground a few yards from General Zy. Four other panthers were either injured or killed, when they got knocked to the ground by the huge blast. A piece of the debris flew up and struck the general on the side of his head, and thereby left him slightly concussed. General Zy was bloodied and wobbled, as if he were about to faint; but maintained his balance and shook it off.

"**Y**ou fool, you have killed us all! What about all those in your village," General Brut shouted to General Zy? "For years you have been supporting this vendetta driven wizard, who cares nothing for you or your kind!"

"General Zy, have some of your panthers secure the shipment, and let's get to the boats," Sorcerer Knoxberry ordered!

"That was not our agreement," General Zy argued!

"It's obvious the plans have changed General! Now get moving," Sorcerer Knoxberry insisted!

"No," General Zy refused!

Without any hesitation Sorcerer Knoxberry fired a metal restraint that bounded his general's hooves together. Loyalists of General Zy were about to attack the sorcerer, when Admiral Tusk stepped between them and stopped them. The plans had indeed changed and without the support of the tigers, Sorcerer Knoxberry had no choice but to include Gybba and his wild boars.

"Are you all not in this for the wealth and power? You heard the wizard, get all the Solar Hibiscus packed crates and let's get off this island," Admiral Tusk ordered!

Some of the panthers refused to leave and chose to defect with General Zy, who was knocked free of the mind control, when the rock struck him in the head. With the lava slowly seeping down the mountainside, Knoxberry had no time to discipline the traitors, thus, anyone who didn't freely join his army got excluded and abandoned.

With Sorcerer Knoxberry, the wild boars, and his panthers racing to their boats on the other side of the island, Taz and the others fought to get their immobilized villagers free. It was impossible to ignore the seeping lava heading toward them, therefore, they either had time to address the immobilized tigers, or the approaching destruction. Most of the Kamoo villagers had ran off in search of refuge from the raging lava, that threatened to destroy the entire Island of Naganoo.

"Leave us and save yourselves," General Brut insisted, after several attempts to free them failed!

"And where will we run to? That lava is going to cover this entire island, and we can't live in the ocean, so we have no other option than to try saving...," Zoah responded, before Sorcerer Knoxberry's abandoned excavation machines gave her an idea. "Everyone come on, we are going to try to save our homeland; or die trying!"

"What do you have in mind," Denny questioned?

"We don't have much time, but I figure if we all use those machines to dig a trench around Mont Plymouth, and lead the lava away from our village, then we might have a chance to survive," Zoah reasoned!

The Volcano King saw the effort being put forth by the Kamoo villagers to save their homes, therefore, he used his powers to reduce the lava velocity, heading toward them. Most of the trenches were barely dug when the lava reached the base of the mountain and gradually filled the gully. Two of the workers who dug the trenches close to Kamoo, were badly scalded, when they waited until the last second, before they exited their excavation machines. As the gully filled, some of the boiling lava managed to breach its banks, and sent the workers frantically running for their lives. The lava that spilt over the edge, travelled along the ground for nearly a mile, before it slowly dried, and came to a stop.

While most of the volunteers worked to complete the trench around Mont Plymouth, others dug another gutter to transport the lava directly to the ocean. There was no time to waste, so every able body resident did their part to save their families, and their island. With nearly a hundred meters left to reach the sea, the villagers found themselves out of time, with the flowing lava at their heels. In their attempt to bring the gutter to the ocean, three panthers and two monkeys paid the ultimate price, when they ignored warnings to evacuate their machines. Most of the flowing lava continued directly to the ocean; however, tons of the molten rocks carved its own path, and transformed most of the island's landscape.

Sorcerer Knoxberry and his followers made it safely to their large boats and immediately began stacking away their cargo. The panthers' village was a few miles away from the docks, and several of the black cats felt they were betraying their families; therefore, they chose to defect and left. The trip to Mukie Island was expected to take a few days, and the wizard could not wait to have his revenge. Despite the defections, Sorcerer Knoxberry still had his robot machine, plus more than enough troops to accomplish his mission, which he was yet to advise the panthers and the boars about.

Admiral Tusk had their workers steadily progressing at a decent pace, and thought they had hours to spare before the lava flow reach their location. The Volcano King was not about to allow them safe passage, with most of his island's resources, so he blew at the slow-moving lava from atop his mountain. The flow of lava began gradually increasing, until it resembled a raging river current, dashing towards the ocean. Sorcerer Knoxberry's cargo stackers were loading their final crates, when one of Gybba's wild boars shouted, "Lava coming!"

Sorcerer Knoxberry ordered his boat captains, 'to take off immediately', therefore they began abandoning the workers still on the docks. The workers being abandoned ran and jumped into the sea, then tried to swim away from the approaching danger, but the scorching lava moved like nothing they had ever seen. The lava came along that entire coastline, then spilt onto the decks of Knoxberry's boats, and into the ocean. The slowly departing boats were set ablaze with the wizard's priceless cargo, thus everyone was forced to abandon the boats. With tons of lava spilling into the ocean, the water quickly began boiling hot with toxic chemicals, that swallowed Sorcerer Knoxberry and his followers.

The panthers that defected from the wizard's army, ran back to their village, and sounded the emergency warning. Once the residents gathered in the square, the defectors warned them about the approaching danger, and what they believed they needed to do to survive. All the panthers were given two-minutes, to return to their homes for survival items they needed, before they all abandoned the village, and escaped to the furthest coastline of Naganoo. The temperature on the island grew increasingly hotter, the closer the horrific molten rocks got to them. As the panthers waited in fear, believing they would perish in the lava, the Volcano King used his powers and stopped the flow, a few yards away from them.

The once beautiful paradise island of Naganoo, looked like a lump of rocks for as far as the eyes could see. The panthers' entire stretch of land was destroyed, so they waited until the lava dried fully, then went in search of survivors and possibly fertile soil on which to live. They walked for hours with both the sun and moonlight, as there were no trees to offer shade. To regain their strength, they rested for three hours then continued along their way. By early afternoon the next day, they reached the land of the Kamoo tigers, and after doubting anything survived, for the first time, they saw dirt, trees, and survivors.

All the surviving species had no choice, but to live in harmony on one fifth of the entire island. The tigers and panthers ended their feud, and began working in unison to feed their families, and protect each other. Every parent began spending more time with their offspring, instead of passing them off to others for care. The most destructive event to ever take place on Naganoo, taught each resident a valid lesson, considering they came close to losing much more than their home.

The reunification of every species on the island, made it once again possible for the Volcano King to teach the youngsters of Naganoo; and his former houseguests were eager to learn more from him. Every other resident on the island, would cringe at the mention of the Volcano King, but the four escapees who knew him best, spoke only of 'wanting to return to his lava kingdom'! Zoah, Taz, Denny, and Jax would climb to the top of Mont Plymouth on the first day of every month from that day forward, until the day the king exposed the ledges, that allowed them to descend into his volcano.

The End

www.ingramcontent.com/pod-product-compliance
Lightning Source LLC
Chambersburg PA
CBHW042316280426
43673CB00080B/394